SOME IMPORTANT PLACES IN SALVADOR DALI'S LIFE

1. **Figueres, Spain**. Salvador Dali was born in this small town in 1904.

2. **Cadaqués, Spain**. A popular vacation spot on the sea. Salvador spent holidays in Cadaqués while growing up. He loved the unusual scenery he saw there. Many of the mysterious backgrounds in Dali's paintings are taken from the deserted seaside areas around Cadaqués.

3. **Madrid, Spain**. Salvador Dali entered the San Fernando Academy of Art in Spain's capital city. At the academy, Dali met poets, writers, and artists who would later become important members of the Surrealist group.

4. **Paris, France**. After leaving art school, Salvador traveled to Paris, the art center of the world. He became friends with famous artists there, including Pablo Picasso. In Paris, Dali started to become well known for his unexpected and sometimes shocking paintings and films.

5. **United States**. Salvador Dali often visited the United States. During and after World War II he lived in New York City and Hollywood, California. He kept busy creating and exhibiting his paintings, and working on movies with many famous filmmakers.

THIS IS THE AREA THAT'S SHOWN ON THE LARGER MAP

RUSSIA · ASIA · China · Japan · India · Alaska · PACIFIC OCEAN · Hawaii · Canada · NORTH AMERICA · U.S.A. · Mexico · ATLANTIC OCEAN · SOUTH AMERICA · EUROPE · Russia · AFRICA · INDIAN OCEAN · AUSTRALIA · N W E S

MAP OF THE ENTIRE TOTAL COMPLETE WORLD · ANTARCTICA

TIMELINE OF SALVADOR DALI'S LIFE

1904 Salvador Dali is born in Figueres, Spain.

1911 Young Salvador begins drawing and painting pictures that show his unusual artistic talent.

1916 During a summer trip to Cadaqués, Dali is introduced to modern art by a local artist.

1917 Dali's father organizes an art show of Salvador's drawings at the family home.

1922 Dali studies painting at the School of Fine Art in Madrid.

1929 Dali moves to Paris and makes his first Surrealist art film. He's invited to join the Surrealist group. He meets Gala, his future wife.

1930 Salvador buys a cottage near Cadaqués, his favorite seaside village.

1931 Dali paints what will become his most famous work, *The Persistence of Memory*.

THIS WAY

UP HERE

1934 Salvador and Gala are married.

1940 Salvador and Gala move to the United States, where they spend eight years befor returning to Europe.

1946 Dali works with Walt Disney on an experimental animated film titled *Destino*.

1952- 1965 Dali keeps very busy writing books and working on art projects. He turns out hundreds of surprising new paintings during this time.

1969 Salvador Dali is super-famou and wealthy. He buys Gala her own ancient stone castle in Spain. He decorates the whole place in his special Salvador Dali style.

1982 The Dali Museum opens in S Petersburg, Florida. It contair one of the largest collections of Salvador Dali work in the world.

1989 Salvador Dali dies of heart failure in Figueres, Spain.

GETTING TO KNOW THE WORLD'S GREATEST ARTISTS

WRITTEN AND ILLUSTRATED BY MIKE VENEZIA

CONSULTANT MEG MOSS

CHILDREN'S PRESS®

An Imprint of Scholastic Inc.

For my surreal son, Michael Anthony

Cover: *Architectonic Angelus of Millet*, 1933. Oil on canvas, 73 x 60 cm. Bridgeman-Giraudon/Art Resource, NY/© ARS, NY.

Library of Congress Cataloging-in-Publication Data

Venezia, Mike.
  Salvador Dali / by Mike Venezia. — Revised Edition.
      pages cm. — (Getting to know the world's greatest artists)
  Includes bibliographical references and index.
  ISBN 978-0-531-21262-2 (library binding) —
  ISBN 978-0-531-21324-7 (pbk.)
  1. Dali, Salvador, 1904-1989—Juvenile literature.
  2. Painters—Spain—Biography—Juvenile literature. I. Title.

ND813.D3V46 2015
709.2—dc23
[B]   2015022173

©2016 by Mike Venezia Inc.

2 3 4 5 6 7 8 9 10 R 25 24 23 22 21 20 19 18 17 16

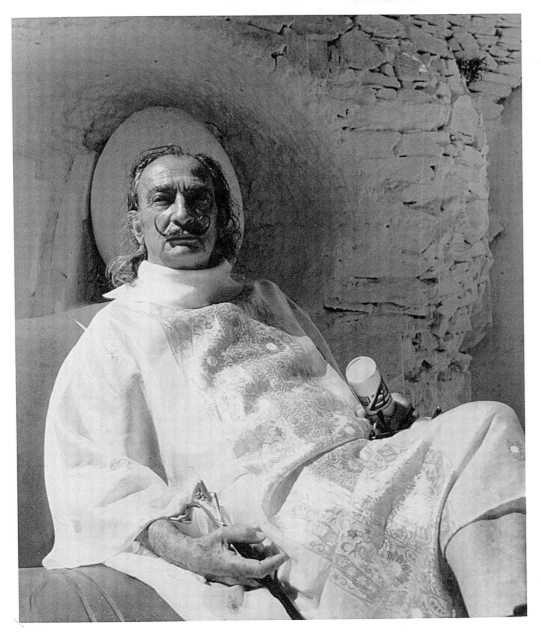

Saint Dali, photograph © Marc Lacroix.
Courtesy of Salvador Dali Museum, St. Petersburg, Florida.

Salvador Dali was born in Figueres, Spain, in 1904. He was one of the most famous and unusual artists of the twentieth century.

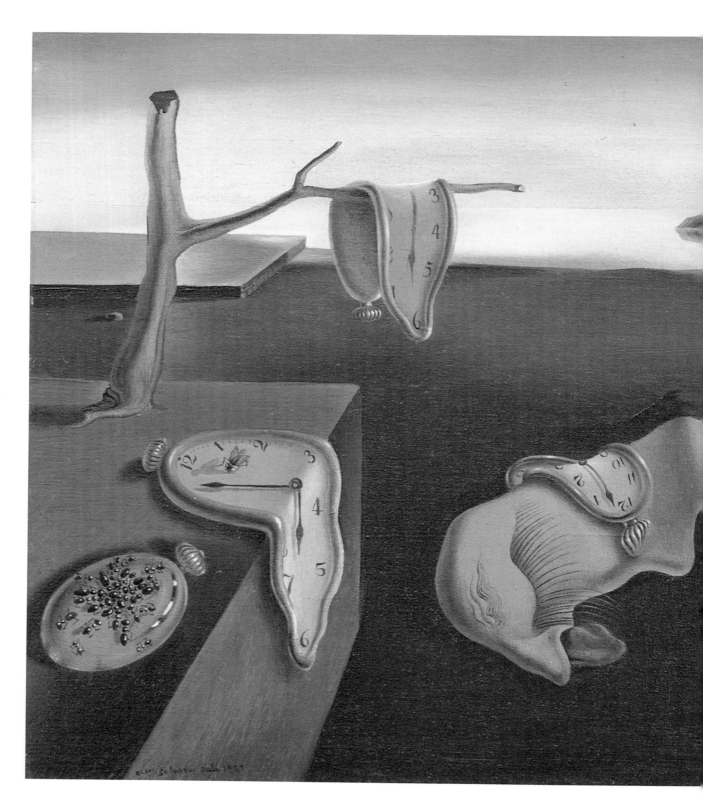

Salvador Dali's best-known paintings are called surrealistic. Most of them are filled with mysterious objects or familiar objects that have been oddly changed.

The Persistence of Memory.
1931. Oil on canvas,
9 ½ x 13 inches.
Collection, The Museum of Modern Art,
New York. Given anonymously.

Even though the things Dali painted look very real, his paintings can be hard to understand. That's because many of the scenes he chose to paint came right out of his dreams.

Metamorphosis of Narcissus.
1934. Oil on canvas,
20 ⅛ x 30 ¾ inches.
Tate Gallery,
London/Art Resource, New York.

Just before Salvador Dali was born, a terrible thing happened to his mother and father. Mr. and Mrs. Dali's first son died. When their new baby arrived, they decided to name him Salvador after the child they had just lost.

They treated the new Salvador as though he were their first son, and were very protective of him.

The second Salvador was very
confused while he was growing up.

Because he was confused, Salvador Dali acted different from other children. He had strange dreams and fears, and he always wanted attention.

Detail of *First Days of Spring*. c. 1929.
Oil on wood panel, 19¾ x 25⅝ inches.
Private collection. Photograph © SuperStock, New York.

Salvador Dali often showed things in his paintings that he remembered from his childhood, even the things that frightened him.

Even after he grew up, Dali kept doing things to get attention, like arriving at an event in a limousine filled with cauliflowers, or giving a talk about his art while wearing a deep-sea diving suit.

He said he received messages from
outer space through his moustache,
which acted like an antenna. People
couldn't wait to see what Salvador
Dali would come up with next.

Cadaques. 1923. Oil on canvas, 37 ⅜ x 49 ⅛ inches.
© Salvador Dali Museum, St. Petersburg, Florida.

While he was growing up, Salvador Dali had a wonderful imagination and was very interested in art. He may have started painting when he was only eight years old, at his family's summer home. The Dali family spent every summer in Cadaqués, Spain, which was right on the sea.

The Weaning of Furniture—Nutrition. 1934. Oil on panel, 7 x 9½ inches.
© Salvador Dali Museum, St. Petersburg, Florida.

Artists from all over would come
to paint the beautiful scenery there.
Some of them were friends of the
Dali family. Salvador Dali loved the
landscape around Cadaqués, and
included scenes he remembered in
many of his later paintings.

When he was a teenager, Salvador went to Madrid, the capital city of Spain, to enter its school of fine arts. Everything seemed fine at first, but soon Salvador got tired of the old-fashioned way art was being taught at the school.

He was more interested in the exciting new art being created in the city of Paris, France. Salvador Dali was especially interested in the paintings of Pablo Picasso, another Spanish artist, who lived in Paris. Dali loved the many new and modern styles of painting that Picasso invented.

Mother and Child. By Pablo Picasso. 1921. Oil on canvas, 56⅖ x 64 inches.
© The Art Institute of Chicago. All Rights Reserved. Gift of Maymar Corporation,
Mrs. Maurice L. Rothschild, Mr. and Mrs. Chauncey McCormick;
Mary and Leigh Block Charitable Fund; Ada Turnbull Hertle Endowment;
through prior gift of Mr. and Mrs. Edwin E. Hokin, 1954.270.

Dali made many trips to Paris. On one of his trips, he got to meet Pablo Picasso.

Venus and Sailor.
By Salvador Dali.
1925. Oil on canvas,
84 3/5 x 58 inches.
Ikeda Museum
of 20th Century Art.
Sizuoka-Ken, Japan.

Some of Dali's early works look
very much like Picasso's paintings
of that time.

Dali also became interested in a group of artists and writers in Paris known as the Surrealists.

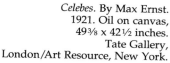

Celebes. By Max Ernst. 1921. Oil on canvas, 49⅜ x 42½ inches. Tate Gallery, London/Art Resource, New York.

Surrealist artists such as Max Ernst, René Magritte, and Joan Miró thought up a whole new way of looking at things.

Time Transfixed. By René Magritte. 1938. Oil on canvas, 57 8/10 x 38 8/10 inches. © The Art Institute of Chicago. All Rights Reserved. Joseph Winterbotham Collection, 1970.426.

The Tilled Field. By Joan Miró. 1923-24. Oil on canvas, 26 x 36 ½ inches.
Solomon R. Guggenheim Museum, New York. FN 72.2020.
Photograph by David Heald, © The Solomon R. Guggenheim Foundation, New York.

They painted mostly what they remembered from their dreams, or anything that automatically popped into their minds. The Surrealists hoped their strange works of art would make people think, and discover feelings they never knew they had. They felt that stirring up thoughts from the backs of people's minds was important for artists to do.

Illumined Pleasures. 1929.
Oil and collage on composition board, 9⅜ x 13¾ inches.
Collection, The Museum of Modern Art, New York.
The Sidney and Harriet Janis Collection.

The Surrealists liked Salvador Dali, and asked him to join their group. Soon he was painting pictures filled with his own dreamlike objects.

The Surrealists thought Dali was such an interesting character that

they sometimes traveled to his home
in Spain to be with him while he
painted. One of the people who
visited him was the wife of a
Surrealist poet. Gala Eluard loved
Dali's work and his unusual
personality.

Gala was very imaginative, too, and liked attention as much as Dali did. Soon, they fell in love. Dali thought Gala was the most beautiful woman in the world, and used her for a model in many of his paintings, like the one on the next page. Gala helped to make sure Salvador Dali and his paintings got noticed as much as possible. Eventually, Gala divorced her husband and married Dali.

Madonna of Port Lligat. 1950.
Oil on canvas, 56 6/10 x 37 7/10 inches.
Lady James Dunn Collection, Canada.
Photograph © SuperStock, New York.

Some of Dali's most famous paintings are very tricky. He often showed that things aren't always what they appear to be at first glance. It's not clear whether the painting on the next page shows a group of people or a statue of the head of a famous French philosopher.

It's kind of like looking at clouds and imagining all the different things you can see in them.

Detail of *Slave Market With Disappearing Bust of Voltaire*. 1940.
Oil on canvas, 18¼ x 25¾ inches.
© Salvador Dali Museum, St. Petersburg, Florida.

Dali's paintings were becoming
well known all over Europe and
America. He wasn't afraid to show
his strangest thoughts or dreams in
his paintings.

Some of the Surrealists felt
that Dali's dreams were too strange.

The Enigma of Hitler. 1939. Oil on canvas. 39 3/10 x 59 inches.
Museo Nacional Centro de Arte Reina Sofía, Madrid, Spain.

They were sometimes offended at what Dali showed, like the cruel dictator, Adolf Hitler, in the painting above. Dali thought this was a ridiculous thing for Surrealists to say and ended up leaving their group. He continued to paint exactly the way he wanted for the rest of his life.

Salvador Dali lived to be eighty-four years old. He is best known for his paintings, but he accomplished many other things during his life.

The Ghost of Vermeer of Delft Which Can Be Used as a Table. 1934. Oil on panel, 7 ⅛ x 5 ½ inches. © Salvador Dali Museum, St. Petersburg, Florida.

Still from the Dali film *L'Age d'or.* 1930. The Museum of Modern Art/Film Stills Archive. New York.

Dali made his own films. He was a very good writer, too. He also designed clothes, fancy perfume bottles, and ads for magazines, and he worked with famous moviemakers in Hollywood, including Walt Disney.

Salvador Dali was always surprising people with his showmanship. He is one of the few great artists who became as famous as his artwork.

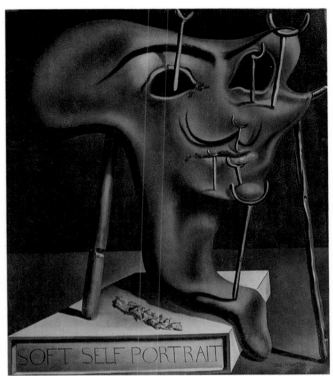

Soft Self-Portrait with Grilled Bacon.
1941. Oil on canvas, 24 1/8 x 20 inches.
Fundació Gala-Salvador Dalí, Figueras, Spain.

Soft Construction with Boiled Beans; Premonition of Civil War. 1936.
Oil on canvas, 39 3/8 x 39 inches.
Philadelphia Museum of Art.
The Louise and Walter Arensberg Collection.

Even though Dali showed his private thoughts in his paintings, they somehow seem familiar, and often remind people of their own private thoughts and dreams.

31

It's fun to see real Salvador Dali paintings close up–they look almost like photographs. Dali usually worked with tiny brushes to make his brush marks as invisible as possible. The paintings in this book came from the museums listed below.

The Art Institute of Chicago, Chicago, Illinois
Fundacío Gala-Salvador Dalí, Figueras, Spain
Ikeda Museum of 20th Century Art, Sizuoka-Ken, Japan
Museo Nacional Centro de Arte Reina Sofía, Madrid, Spain
The Museum of Modern Art, New York, New York
Philadelphia Museum of Art, Philadelphia, Pennsylvania
Salvador Dali Museum, St. Petersburg, Florida
The Solomon R. Guggenheim Museum, New York, New York
Tate Gallery, London, England

LEARN MORE BY TAKING THE DALI QUIZ!

(ANSWERS ON THE NEXT PAGE.)

1. Aside from his Surrealist paintings, Salvador Dali was also known for:
   a. Writing books
   b. Making surreal art films
   c. Being a respected little-league coach
   d. Fashion, jewelry, and furniture designs
   e. Strange and weird behavior

2. What were some favorite objects Salvador Dali showed over and over in his paintings?
   a. Slices of anchovy pizza, cell phones, comic-book super heroes, and BBQ grills
   b. Eggs, melting watches, ants, crutches, and loaves of bread
   c. 1968 Corvette Stingrays, Barcelona chairs, polar bears, and tomato-soup cans

3. Who were some important Hollywood filmmakers Salvador Dali worked with?
   a. Alfred Hitchcock
   b. Walt Disney
   c. The Marx Brothers
   d. George Lucas

4. Salvador Dali was very fond of animals. For many years he owned a pet Ocelot. What is an Ocelot?
   a. A species of giant anteater
   b. A rare African python
   c. A type of wild cat

5. What were some of Salvador Dali's favorite foods?
   a. Any type of shellfish, including lobster, shrimp, oysters, and crayfish
   b. Simmered eel with bacon and soybeans topped with cream
   c. Frozen chocolate bananas on a stick
   d. Snails, frog legs, and Camembert cheese

ANSWERS

1. a, b, d, & e Salvador Dali was known for all kinds of creative projects and activities, including his strange and weird behavior!

2. b All of these objects were things that came from Salvador Dali's dreams, childhood memories, and worst fears.

3. a, b, & c Aside from creating his own artsy films, Dali worked with a number of famous award-winning filmmakers, including Alfred Hitchcock, Walt Disney, and the Marx Brothers.

4. c An Ocelot is a spotted wild cat similar to a small leopard. Dali's Ocelot was named Babou. If someone was afraid of Dali's pet, he would tell them Babou was just a regular cat that he painted with spots.

5. a, b, & d When Salvador Dali was six years old, he told people he wanted to be a cook. Dali always enjoyed preparing unusual dishes. In 1973, he wrote and illustrated a cookbook for Gala that included many strange and original recipes.

HEY, WHAT DOES THAT WORD MEAN?

antenna (an-TEN-uh) A wire that receives radio and television signals

cauliflower (KAW-luh-flou-ur) A vegetable with a large, rounded white head

dictator (DIK-tay-tur) Someone who has complete control of a country, often ruling it unjustly

imagination (i-maj-uh-NAY-shuhn) The ability to form pictures in your mind of things that are not present or real

model (MOD-uhl) Someone who poses for an artist

modern (MOD-urn) To do with the present or the recent past

mysterious (miss-TIHR-ee-uhss) Very hard to explain or understand

philosopher (fuh-LOSS-uh-fuhr) Someone who studies truth, wisdom, and the nature of reality

ridiculous (ri-DIK-yuh-luhss) Extremely silly or foolish

showmanship (SHOH-muhn-ship) The ability to do things in a lively and enthusiastic way that attracts attention

Visit this Scholastic Web site for more information on Dali:
www.factsfornow.scholastic.com
Enter the keyword **Dali**

INDEX